GW00870493

AWESOME BANK

DATE: _____

PAY TO THE
ORDER OF: _____ $ [ ]

_____ DOLLARS

FOR: _____

⑆000000151⑆ 000000000 ⑈296⑆ 457

AWESOME BANK

DATE: _____

PAY TO THE
ORDER OF: _____ $ [ ]

_____ DOLLARS

FOR: _____

⑆000000151⑆ 000000000 ⑈296⑆ 457

AWESOME BANK

DATE: _____

PAY TO THE
ORDER OF: _____ $ [ ]

_____ DOLLARS

FOR: _____

⑆000000151⑆ 000000000 ⑈296⑆ 457

Checks are pieces of paper used to make payments.

PRACTICE ONLY

I've lost my tail.

A story by

Terry and Phoenix Mack.

As you might guess,
Phoenix was
a tall and
fearsome
tyrannosaurus rex.

His favourite things to do all day are to run..

Phoenix was not
feeling himself today.

What was so different?
It was hard to say.

OH NO! He cried.
I'VE LOST MY TAIL.

He ran to his room, but It wasn't there, he looked high and low, it wasn't anywhere.

I've lost my tail; it went so fast.
I can't remember where I saw it last.

He roared to the living room where his brother,
the grouch,
was there looking grumpy
slumped on the couch.

I've lost my tail; where could it be?
It's usually right here following me.

Brother!
You're no help
at all. You'd
only care if
it was your
basketball.

He heard his sister on the garden swing;
he jumped on his scooter
and shot off with a zing.

I've lost my tail; it must be near.
I may never find it;
I'm starting to fear.

Phoenix went off to find Mum and Dad,
to tell them about losing the tail he once had.

I've lost my tail;
I'm in quite a pickle.
I miss the way that
it used to tickle.

I miss how I could make it go thwack.
And how it went all the way from
the floor to my back.

I've lost my tail,
it's come
undone.

Time to search
for it?
I have none

As night drew near, he had to rest his head;
Phoenix and his family went off to bed.

He pulled back his blanket, and there plain to see
was his long green tail, which filled him with glee.

How did it get
here?
Magic perhaps?
Although it falls
off sometimes
when I'm taking
my naps.

As Dad ensured Phoenix
was tightly tucked in;
mum carefully attached his
tail with a pin.

As Phoenix fell asleep, a thought entered his head.

Next time the first place I'll look is my bed.

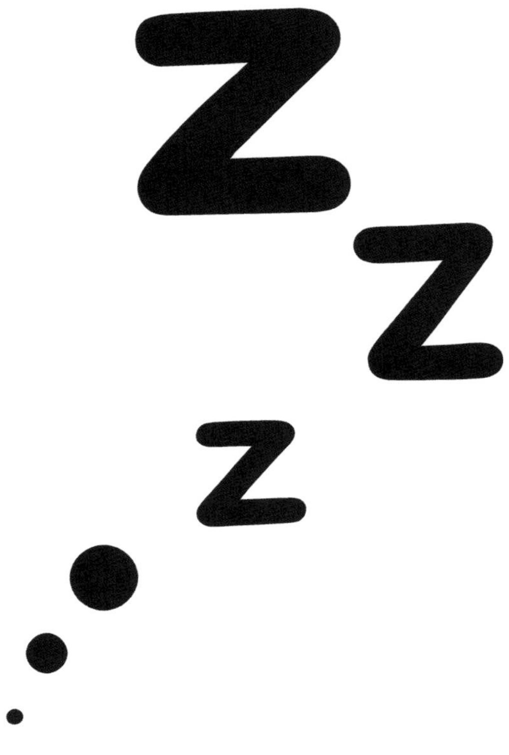
Zzz

The End

**Original ideas
from the beautiful mind of
Phoenix Mack**

How this story was created

Phoenix loves nothing more than reading
or having stories read to him.
One day he asked to have a story that he was in, so we played
around with lots of silly stories including his friends and family.
We kept coming back to the story of Phoenix the dinosaur
losing his tail. I started writing it down so as not to forget any
details and it grew from there.

This is still one of his favourite stories to read.

Printed in Great Britain
by Amazon